Laura Land, POPULATION TWO

❧

Laura Amalfitano

To order additional copies of this book, contact:
Xlibris
844-714-8691
www.Xlibris.com
Orders@Xlibris.com

ISBN: *Softcover*   *978-1-6641-6298-3*
          EBook   *978-1-6641-6297-6*

Print information available on the last page

Rev. date: 03/12/2021

Dedicated to Dana, the nicest and most genuine person I know, and to Dominic and Dimitri, who find ways to show kindness every day.

Laura Shutts grew up in South Portland, Maine. The youngest of five children and the only girl, she learned at a young age how important it is to share and respect other people's space. She was raised by two hard working parents, who gave her more than they ever believed they had. Laura went on to live in York, Pennsylvania, where she raised her three children and spent many hours volunteering at school and cheering the children on at sporting events. Today she works as an insurance agent, and spends her free time with her family and friends, whom she cherishes more than anything in the world.

Always do the right thing, especially when it is not easy. You won't ever regret it, and will be able to sleep at night.

❧

Try to be aware of your surroundings, and be courteous to the people around you when you are in public. We all live in this world together and must share the public spaces.

Always say thank you when someone holds the door for you. It's really easy to do, and should come naturally to you after a while.

❧

Give a smile to a stranger. People will appreciate your kindness, and it will make you feel good inside.

Make people laugh whenever you can.
Everybody enjoys laughter and it is good for the soul.

~∽

Always help someone when you see an opportunity. Most people won't ask for help, but they will be so grateful for the help they receive.

❦

Be a good listener. Sometimes people just need to talk, and a kind ear to listen.

❧

Make someone feel welcome when they are new to the environment and do not know anyone. Be their first friend.

༼ ༽

You don't have to be the biggest or the best, just be the nicest.

If you have small children, teach them to be kind. They will become kind adults, and the world needs all the kindness it can get.

If you have young athletes, cheer only in a positive manner at sporting events.
Don't be critical of your athlete or other athletes. They just want to play the game.

❧

Try to be sensitive to others, and think about what they might be dealing with in their lives. Everybody has a story to tell.

⁊

Don't let discussions about politics cause conflict with friends, co-workers, or family members. It's not important enough to ruin relationships over.

❧

It is always best to tell the truth, and it's easier to live with yourself if you do, even if it doesn't seem easy at the time.

*If you have a family, be grateful every day. Be faithful
and loyal to them, above all things.*

If you are lucky enough to have somebody to love who loves you back, don't take them for granted. Be thoughtful and respectful at all times, because some people are not as lucky.

Be a good friend, even if distance between you makes it difficult.
A good friend is one of life's most precious gifts.

Just be a regular person. You don't have to pretend to be someone you're not, who you are is good enough.

Live simply. You don't need expensive cars, clothing, or possessions to have a good life. You will find that you can live with very little.

☙

Be kind to the earth. Don't waste water or electricity, only use what you need, and recycle whatever you can.

❧

Treat everyone the same. Don't treat people differently based on their appearance.

☙

Don't be a know-it-all. You can't possibly know everything about everything.

❧